MW01235844

HOLY SPIRIT

AGENT OF CHANGE

Loretta Huggins

WORD & SPIRIT
PUBLISHING

HOLY SPIRIT: AGENT OF CHANGE
Copyright 2022 by Loretta Huggins
ISBN: 978-1-949106-87-9

Published by Word and Spirit Publishing
P.O. Box 701403
Tulsa, Oklahoma 74170
wordandspiritpublishing.com

---

[1] To learn more about the fourteenth-century Bible scholar John Wycliffe, and why his translation of the Bible is historically important visit these two websites: https://www. britannica.com/biography/John-Wycliffe and https://www.christianitytoday.com/ history/people/moversandshakers/john-wycliffe.html.

Endorsements

"Holy Spirit-Agent of Change" is full of personal, practical accounts that drew me in as if I was actually present in each story Loretta tells. Loretta is not only articulate in her writing, but her personal knowledge of the Holy Spirit, as her Helper, makes you want to jump right into this kind of relationship—an adventure in life with the Holy Spirit, and what an adventure it is!

"This book is full of Scriptural references, which makes this book perfect for your personal Bible Study on the Holy Spirit, small group or home gathering. We all need continual change and we are all in the process of continual transformation—from one degree of glory to another and the Agent of change lives in us!

This book will be part of my "keeper" library. I encourage every reader to make it part of theirs!

> — Pr. Verna Del Turco
>   co-founding pastor of International Family Church
>   North Reading, MA

Get ready for Scriptures, precise word origins, and applications, personal experiences, warm bits of nostalgic application. That will usher you into an expanded understanding of the work and personal interaction of the Holy Spirit of Jehovah God and His work as your helper in the everyday ups and downs of the normal Christian life. As you read you will be strengthened in your inner man. Thank you Loretta Huggins for this notable contribution to the more perfect understanding of the Gospel. I quote; Many daughters have done virtuous, as have you.

— Dr John F Avanzini
Founder and president of
John Avanzini International Ministries

"I have known Loretta Huggins for over 30 years. Her love of the Holy Spirit was evident from the first conversation I had with her. I've read several wonderful books on this timely subject but none better , in my opinion, then this "Gem " Pastor Loretta has written. Get ready to be encouraged and blessed!

— Dick Bernal
Founder/Pastor of Jubilee Christian Center/
Jubilee Legacy International

Dedication

In loving memory of my mother,
Marie M. Washington,
who taught me to love the Holy Spirit

Contents

Acknowledgments

This book would not have been possible without the loving support of my husband, Larry W. Huggins, who for many years encouraged me to write. During the process of writing this book, he read the rough, second, third, and fourth drafts of my manuscript, offering content and grammar advice.

My son, Yusef U. Terry, also encouraged me to write. His many pep talks were a source of inspiration, and his constant inquiries on my progress were the impetus I needed.

After reading my rough draft, Paula B. Flood, my BBF (beautiful best friend), offered valuable advice and support that only a BBF can give.

My mentors, Dr. John Avanzini and the late Pastor Patricia Avanzini, are lovers of the Holy Spirit—they have invested much into my life.

Thank you!

Foreword

I learned something from this little book that made a big change in my prayer life. You know how it is when we see something we've never seen, and we say to ourselves, "Now, this changes everything"?

Let me illustrate what I mean. What does everyone eat when they visit New England? Lobster, of course. It's on the menu in almost every eatery. When people are in Boston, they expect to get good lobster. My friend took me to Jimmy's on the Back Bay. He said, "You like lobster, right? Let me order a lobster dish for you that's not on the menu." He called the chef over to his table and whispered his order. A few minutes later came the dish the chef was famous for: fried lobster. It was thinly sliced, lightly breaded, and fried in butter.

That dish changed everything for me. After that, every time I visited Boston, I would invite my friends to Jimmy's, and I'd say, "You like lobster, right? Let me order for you." Most cooks prepare ordinary things. But chefs create extraordinary things.

For example, I've preached countless times from Loretta's text for this book, Romans 8:26–29. It's been a staple of my ministry. Honestly I thought I'd squeezed the last drop of juice from those grapes. Then, my dear wife dropped the same cluster of Scriptures into her press. Voilà! Out flowed new wine.

Let me take my analogy a bit further. Good preaching is like good cooking. That's why I see this little book as a cookbook. It's not just informative—it's nourishing. Each chapter is a recipe for success. Taken together, it provides a feast for the soul.

Once, in West Africa, a man complimented my preaching. He said, "Brother Huggins, I like the way you cook!" Now it's my turn to pay my compliments to our chef. "Sister Huggins, I like the way you cook!" Yes, this changes everything.

—Larry Huggins

Likewise the Spirit also helpeth our infirmities: for we know not what we should pray for as we ought: but the Spirit itself maketh intercession for us with groanings which cannot be uttered. And he that searcheth the hearts knoweth what is the mind of the Spirit, because he maketh intercession for the saints according to the will of God. And we know that all things work together for good to them that love God, to them who are the called according to his purpose.

—ROMANS 8:26–28

Preface

Why Another Book about
the Holy Spirit?

A simple search on one of the most popular search engines will render a plethora of information on the Holy Spirit, ranging from short essays to hardbound books. For instance, one of the world's largest sites for readers and book recommendations provides a must-read list comprised of fifty-four books about the Holy Spirit, including the Holy Bible. (No recommended reading about the Holy Spirit is complete without the Holy Bible!) Also, multiple sites dedicated to a particular religious sect or special-interest group provide hundreds of essays dating back to the 1900s on the Holy Spirit.

With this in mind, you may wonder why we need another book on the Holy Spirit? Perhaps you may even argue that the subject of the Holy Spirit—that is, *who* and *why* is He—has been exhausted. What possible new information or revision of information about the Spirit of God would make this book worth the time to read? The best way to answer that question is to use a popular clichéd term: *game changer.*

The straightforward meaning of the phrase *game changer* is this: "an event, idea, or procedure that affects a significant shift in the current way of doing or thinking about something." To add to that meaning, a game changer is "something or someone that dramatically changes the outcome of a given situation."[2] The following are examples of different types of technology that changed everything in their wake.[3]

 The 1912 Model T: Even though Gottlieb Daimler[4] invented the high-speed liquid petroleum-fueled engine in the late 1800s, Henry Ford's 1912 Model T Roadster was the game changer for the ordinary American. Ford mass-produced the Model T, making it possible for the average American to own an automobile.[5]

---

2 See https://www.merriam-webster.com/dictionary/game%20changer.

3 See https://www.pcworld.com/article/508115/tech_gamechangers.html.

4 See https://www.daimler.com/company/tradition/founders-pioneers/gottlieb-daimler.html.

5 1912 Model T Roadster; image courtesy of the Henry Ford Museum.

Zenith Flash-Matic TV Remote: Oh my, I am old enough to remember television viewing before the convenience of a remote control. The introduction of Flash-Matic in 1955 was a game changer for in-home entertainment; before its introduction, the television viewer had to change the TV channels manually by turning knobs on the TV.[6]

 Motorola DynaTAC 8000X: Measuring more than 12 inches long, weighing more than 2 pounds, and costing $4,000, introduced in 1983 and immortalized in the 1987 blockbuster movie *Wall Street,* was the first commercially available untethered cell phone. This "outdated" model was the game changer in how, when, what, and where we communicate with others today.[7]

Before Ford's Model T, Zenith's Flash-Matic, and Motorola's DynaTAC cell phone, people traveled, enjoyed in-home entertainment, and communicated with one another; however, those inventions were (and still are) the *game changers* in how we do all of these things today.

In the same manner, this book offers a new and dynamic way to understand the role of the Holy Spirit in a believer's

---

[6] Photo courtesy of TV History; see http://tvhistory.tv/index.html.

[7] Motorola DynaTAC; see http://content.time.com/time/specials/packages/article/0,28804,2023689_2023708_2023656,00.html

life. The information contained in this book can change every situation in your life in a significant way—so that you can *"move from one brighter level of glory to another"* (2 Corinthians 3:18 TPT).

The Holy Spirit can change you from
victim to *victor*—
He is the Agent of Change!

Introduction

We Could Have Handled That Better

$\mathcal{O}$ne of my favorite movies is the 2002 blockbuster *The Count of Monte Cristo*,[8] based on Alexandre Dumas' novel by the same name.[9] In the movie version, Edmond Dantès, the protagonist, and his cellmate, Faria, the priest, dig an underground tunnel to escape the horrible prison Château d'If.[10] One day, while digging, there is a cave-in, and Faria is fatally injured. Before Faria dies, he instructs Edmond to keep digging, abandon his desire for vengeance, and follow God's teaching. Edmond refuses. Later, during the nightly routine cell-check,

---

[8] See *The Count of Monte Cristo*, https://en.wikipedia.org/wiki/The_Count_of_Monte_Cristo_(2002_film).

[9] See Alexandre Dumas, https://www.biography.com/writer/alexandre-dumas.

[10] Château d'If is regarded as one of the most famous European prisons. For more about the historic prison, visit http://www.prisonhistory.net/famous-prisons/chateau-dif-prison/.

two jailers discover that Faria is dead. They place the dead priest into a body bag. Then they leave the body unattended to go and tell the warden of the prisoner's death. Before the jailers return with the warden, Edmond secretly trades places with the dead priest. The jailers carry the body bag, as the warden follows, to the cliffs of the prison island. Unbeknownst to them, Edmond is in the body bag instead of the dead priest. As the warden thoughtlessly mumbles the words of the last rites, the jailers prepare to toss the body bag over the cliff into the surrounding sea by swinging it back and forth. Just before the jailers release the body bag into the air, Edmond sticks his hand through a small opening and grabs the warden by the belt. To the jailers' surprise, the warden goes flying over the cliff with the body bag into the treacherous waters below. The dumbstruck jailers watch in disbelief from the edge of the cliff as Edmond frees himself from the chain-wrapped body bag and then exacts revenge on the evil warden. After the drama is over, the warden sinks to the bottom of the sea, and Edmond swims toward freedom, one jailer then looks at the other jailer and says, *"You know, we could have handled that better."*

It is safe to say that everyone has experienced such an unpleasant could-have-handled-that-better moment in life. The jailers did not have all the facts, and neither you nor I will ever have all the facts about any given situation in our lives. We will always experience some form of handicap in our decision-making process due to the limitations of our knowledge and understanding about an issue; therefore, we need help to make the best decisions possible. The Holy Spirit, sent by God the Father, is the Spirit of Truth, given to us at the request of Christ Jesus.

And I will pray the Father, and he shall give you another Comforter, that he may abide with you for ever; even the Spirit of truth.

—JOHN 14:16–17

In Greek, Jesus Christ called the Holy Spirit the *parakletos*, which means in English the following:

- Advocate: one who speaks or writes in support or defense of a person or cause
- Counselor: one who counsels and advises
- Consoler: one who alleviates or lessens another's grief, sorrow, or disappointment and gives solace or comfort
- Intercessor: one who intercedes (acts or interposes[11]) on behalf of someone in difficulty, reconciles differences between two or more people, and mediates
- Succorer: one who helps, relieves, aids, and assists
- Aider: one who promotes the progress or accomplishments of another
- Assistant: one who supplements, that is, completes, adds to, or extends

---

[11] *Interpose* is an interesting word, meaning "to place between, to intervene, to be a mediator in a conversation or discourse."

In life, every person will need support, defense, advice, comfort, assistance, and so much more. Yes, you and I have family, friends, mentors, and others we trust to speak into our lives; however, those persons are as we are. They, too, are limited by their inability to know all there is to know about all that concerns a given issue. Everyone is biased toward family, friends, and so forth. And everyone can be biased against others who are considered "different." Our preferences are often based on inaccurate or incomplete information. That is why we need the Agent of Change, the Holy Spirit, in our lives. He will help us make the right decisions based on the truth.

This truth changes everything!

1

A Person, Not an "It"

*Likewise the Spirit also helpeth our infirmities: for
we know not what we should pray for as we ought:
but the Spirit itself maketh intercession for us with
groanings which cannot be uttered.*

—ROMANS 8:26

*T*he King James Bible renders the Greek word *autos* as
"itself"; however, in both the *Strong's Concordance*[12] and the

---

[12] *James Strong's Exhaustive Concordance* is the most complete and easy-to-use
tool for studying the original languages of the Bible. See https://www.bible-
studytools.com/concordances/strongs-exhaustive-concordance/.

Thayer's Greek-English Lexicon,[13] the translation of *autos* includes all the reflexive pronouns: *myself, yourself, himself, herself, oneself, itself, ourselves, and themselves.* Why the sixteenth-century King James translators chose to use *itself* instead of *himself* is a mystery to me. They certainly had the same second-century and fourth-century manuscripts available to them, as did both nineteenth-century Bible scholars James Strong (1822–1894)[14] and Joseph Henry Thayer (1828–1901).[15] The King James Version (KJV) is the most popular Bible in Western culture. Based on its translation of the Greek word *autos,* some view the Spirit as an "it." In the English dictionary, the word *it* has as its first shade of definition: "to represent an inanimate thing."[16] The word *inanimate* means "sluggish, dull, lifeless, and spiritless."

It is not possible for the Spirit of Life to be lifeless and spiritless. In modern English, the word *it* is used as a substitute for the pronouns *he* and *she*; however, using *it* to refer to a person is offensive. In Old English, the word *it* was used to reference a

---

[13] Joseph Henry Thayer's *Greek-English Lexicon of the New Testament* is one of the greatest achievements in biblical scholarship at the turn of the twentieth century (https://www.logos.com/).

[14] To learn about James Strong and his works, follow this link: http://www.bible-tools123.com/Who-Was-James-Strong.

[15] To learn about Joseph Henry Thayer and his works, follow this link: https://www.journals.uchicago.edu/doi/pdfplus/10.1086/472978.

[16] Dictionary.com is an online dictionary whose domain was first registered on May 14, 1995. The content for Dictionary.com is based on the latest version of *Random House Unabridged Dictionary,* with editors for the site providing new and updated definitions.

he-goat.[17] (In Old, Middle, and Modern English, to refer to a person as an "it" is disrespectful.) A thought to ponder: If we are the sheep of God's pasture, would there not be a conflict of interest if the Spirit of God has the nature of a he-goat?

[Jesus said,] When the Son of man shall come . . . he shall separate . . . [the] sheep from the goats . . . the sheep on his right hand, but the goats on the left . . . Then shall the King say [to those] on his right hand . . . ye [are] blessed . . . then . . . unto them on [his] left hand, Depart from me.

—MATTHEW 25:31–46

Sadly, referring to the Holy Spirit as *it* is not the only misconception many people have of God's Spirit. Case in point, the Holy Spirit has been referred to as wind, breath, water, fire, and even a bird.[18] Those descriptions and others, such as *the voice of God,*[19] are similes and metaphors, which are rhetorical devices. Such devices are linguistic tools used to evoke memories, feelings, and associations to get a reaction from an audience. To further explain, when speakers or writers are describing the nature of someone or something, they will sometimes use a comparison to give their audience a *reference point,* which can arouse the audience's emotions.

---

[17] For more information about the definition of *it*, follow this link: https://www.etymonline.com/word/it.

[18] Reference Scriptures include wind (Acts 2:2); breath (Ezekiel 37:9); water (John 4:14; 7:38); fire (Acts 2:3; Matthew 3:11); bird (Matthew 3:16).

[19] The Voice of God (Genesis 3:8; Psalm 29:3).

In everyday life, we use different forms of rhetorical devices. For instance, someone once told me that he felt as if he had been hit by a loaded Mack truck traveling at highway speeds to impress upon me how much pain he was experiencing. His statement was an exaggeration: He used the rhetorical device of *hyperbole*. Suppose he had been hit by a loaded semitruck, which can weigh upwards of 80,000 pounds[20]; suffice it to say that he and I would not have been having that conversation. The initial impact of the Mack truck would have also been followed by its 50-foot-plus trailer running over him. His description of how he felt was quite an exaggeration. How often have you heard someone state, "I just died," or "I was completely mortified"? If the person had actually died, then either you are communicating with a ghost, or you, both, are in the After-life. Those statements are simply ways of amplifying how the speaker feels.

Did you know that *humor* is a rhetorical device that most likely everyone uses in everyday life? Humor creates connection and identification between people; humor can also deflate an escalating situation. I am reminded of an incident that involved my husband and a police officer. My husband and I were traveling from San Francisco International Airport (SFO) to Chicago O'Hare International Airport (ORD). Our destination was Rushville, Illinois, about a three-hour drive from the Chicago airport. We arrived in Chicago around 10:30 p.m. We were tired from the five-hour flight packed with rude passengers and

---

[20] For Mack Truck info, see https://www.macktrucks.com/trucks/granite-series/specs/.

crying babies. By the time we retrieved our luggage and secured a rental car, it was close to midnight.

To repeat, we were tired. Worn out and sleepy, my husband was motivated to reach our destination in less than three hours. An hour out of Rushville, as we were clipping along at a good rate of speed, out of nowhere, a police car appeared behind us with flashing lights and a screeching siren. Larry pulled over to the side of the road and let out a deep groan. It was about 2:00 a.m. The police car stopped behind us. The blinding, bright white lights on the patrol car flooded our vehicle. Larry rolled down the driver's-side window and waited for the officer to approach the car. Armed with a flashlight, the officer aimed it first at me, then at Larry. With the flashlight trained on Larry's face, the officer asked him, "Is that your wife, or what?"

When I heard the officer's words, I started quietly praying in the Holy Spirit! That was a good decision because my husband was annoyed at the police's offensive question. Larry answered the officer in a quiet but firm voice, "She is my wife." At that point, the officer asked another question: "Do you know why I stopped you?" Neither the officer nor I was prepared for my husband's reply: "To make new friends?" The officer and my husband stared at one another for what seemed like an eternity. Sitting in the passenger's side of the vehicle, I continued to pray in the Holy Spirit. Then the officer chuckled a bit and said, "Well, I guess that's better than making enemies." Larry's sense of humor deflated the situation.

The following day, we shared with our host couple what had happened to us en route to their home. Happily, we added that the officer did not issue Larry a traffic ticket. Our hosts' eyes widened in amazement. They explained to us that it was a miracle that Larry did not receive a traffic ticket because that area, which is about twenty miles south of Rushville, Illinois, was featured on one of the popular television investigation programs as a notorious speed trap.

The point I am making is that long before the definition of *rhetoric* was narrowed into the modern view that it is just for debates and arguments, these devices were (and still are) used in everyday speech. We marvel at the abilities of great writers, such as Geoffrey Chaucer (1343-1400),[21] William Shakespeare (1564-1616), Paul Dunbar Laurence (1872-1906),[22] and Maya Angelou (1928-2014). They used literary devices to challenge their readers to examine their thoughts and beliefs by painting powerful images with words. For example, Maya Angelou's "Still I Rise"[23] is an excellent example of various rhetorical devices, as she conveys to the reader that she will always *rise as the victor despite adverse opposition!* Does the Bible not state the very same message?

---

[21] Chaucer's birth year is guesstimated between 1340 and 1343.

[22] Paul Dunbar Laurence is one of the first African American poets to gain national recognition. To learn more about his life and works, follow these links: https://poets.org/poet/paul-laurence-dunbar; short bio-video of his life: https://youtu.be/So2tXW2oS2M.

[23] For information about "Still I Rise" by Maya Angelou, follow this link: https://www.poetryfoundation.org/poems/46446/still-i-rise.

*Do you think anyone is going to be able to drive a wedge
between us and Christ's love for us? There is no way! . . .
They kill us in cold blood. . . . We're sitting ducks. . . .*[24]
*But no matter what comes, we will always taste victory
through [Christ].*[25]

—ROMANS 8:35–37

Note the rhetorical devices used in the above Scripture
passage: *Drive a wedge, in cold blood, sitting ducks,* and *taste of
victory* are all literary devices to powerfully convey the message
of *being a winner in Christ* despite any opposition. When I read
the above Scripture passage, I understand that no one, no situation, and nothing can stop Christ from loving me. Even if the
situation that I am in seems hopeless, to the extent that I feel as
if I am a sitting duck with the crosshairs of a rifle trained on me,
I will still be the victor. Ahhh, the sweet taste of victory! (And
no, it doesn't taste like chicken.)[26]

Interestingly, Jesus Christ referred to Himself as *the Bread
of Life:* "Verily, verily, I say unto you . . . I am that bread of life . . .
the living bread which came down from heaven" (John 6:47–51).
Yet it is safe to surmise that no one has ever had the mental
picture of Jesus depicted as a big loaf of bread descending out

---

[24] This portion is copied from *The Message.*
[25] This portion is copied from *The Voice.*
[26] "Simile, humorous" describes the taste of unique foods that are hard to describe
by comparing it to the blandness of chicken, because chicken can taste like
anything.

of heaven. Nor has anyone depicted Jesus Christ as an illuminated vine bursting forth from the ground; He did state in John 15:1, "I am the true vine." Plus, John the Baptist called Jesus *"the Lamb of God"* (John 1:29). Even though Christ is portrayed in countless paintings and drawings as a delicate lamb resting in a flower bed, is He really a four-footed animal?

You may think my examples are bordering on the verge of sacrilegious. It is just the opposite. My reasoning is meant to prove that it is just as absurd to view the Holy Spirit as a he-goat, timid bird, or running water as it is to depict Jesus Christ as a floating loaf of bread. Again, all of these references are types of rhetorical devices, meant to help us understand the nature of Christ and of the Holy Spirit. To repeat, you and I use sayings and phrases to create images in the minds of others.

To belabor my point, when I was a teenager, I heard a woman say that there was nothing in the drugstore strong enough to kill someone quicker than she could: Her words evoked a frightful image in my mind.

Who knows more about how to use words to create a powerful image in a person's mind—life-changing images—than the Spirit of Truth? Look at Matthew 3:16: "And Jesus, when he was baptized, went up straightway out of the water: and, lo, the heavens were opened unto him, and he saw the Spirit of God descending like a dove, and lighting upon him." The phrase *"descending like a dove"* simulates how the Spirit appeared on Christ. Note that the Scripture does not read, *"the Spirit of God, a dove, descended on Jesus."*

Most people think of a dove as a timid and gentle bird because it walks as if its feet are tender—lightly stepping as it goes about its life. The dove is a gentle bird that coos softly and flies gracefully; however, the dove is also known for its fast, powerful, precise flight patterns and the sharp, whirling sound created by its wings.[27] Thus, Matthew 3:16 describes the powerful precision of the anointing of the Holy Spirit, whirling the atmosphere with His presence as He hovered over Jesus. Acts 2:2 gives another account of the Holy Spirit stirring the atmosphere with His presence: *"Without warning there was a sound like a strong wind, gale force"* (MSG). Be assured that the Holy Spirit will never miss the mark when it comes to filling you with His presence. His presence will always change the atmosphere. He is the most powerful presence in the world today. He is the third person of the Trinity. He has come to help us become *more than conquerors* in Christ, providing us with power and insight to live as victors. Anointed by the Holy Spirit, Jesus Christ referred to the Spirit as a *He*: "Howbeit when he, the Spirit of truth, is come, he will guide you into all truth" (John 16:13). Knowing what is *true* in any matter under consideration is a *life-changer*.

Jesus continued to state in John 16 that the Spirit of Truth will guide us and tell us what He has heard from God. Water, wind, or a bird cannot tell you or me what God is saying to us in a language we understand. You and I may experience the presence of the Spirit as water flooding over us. Or we may

---

[27] To learn more about the characteristics of a dove, visit https://sciencing.com/characteristics-doves-8686274.html.

experience His presence as wind blowing on us. We may even experience His presence gently lighting upon us like a dove. But just remember that He is God the Spirit. He is in our lives to guide us into what is true in any matter under consideration. One of the hallmarks of the Spirit of Truth is precision. You and I need His help to know God's plans for our lives. Why else would we pray if we are not seeking God's will? Too often, the focus of our prayers is to make God's will fit into our own desires and plans instead of yielding our desires and plans to the will of God. It is easy to disobey an inanimate entity; however, if we are to avoid future "oh no" moments as much as possible, then we must have Him, the Spirit *of exactness,* informing us in all issues of our lives.

The *precision* of the Holy Spirit
changes everything!

2

Likewise, *to What?*

Likewise the Spirit also helpeth our infirmities.

—ROMANS 8:26

*W*hile writing this book, I wondered about the connection between the word *likewise* in Romans 8:26 and the preceding verses. The transition between verses 25 and 26 did not make sense, because the word *likewise* means "in the same way, in like manner, or in addition to." What is being referenced by the word *likewise*? The Spirit helps us in *like manner* compared to what? It seemed to me that the apostle Paul's letter to the Romans began to lack cohesiveness, possibly starting with chapter 6, derailing in chapter 7, and "falling apart" by chapter

8. I thought the apostle Paul had tried to make too many points without making clear connections. The first part of Romans deals with the Gospel of Christ, and then bad life choices, then on to the faith of Abraham. Then chapters 6 and 7 state the traps of the carnal flesh. As if the first seven chapters of Romans did not present more than enough topics to contemplate, in the subsequent thirty-nine verses of the eighth chapter of Romans, the apostle Paul introduces at least seventeen more subjects:

- Freedom from condemnation
- The law of life versus the law of death
- Christ's fulfillment of the law's requirements
- The carnal mind versus the mind of the Spirit
- Adoption/sonship versus servitude/slavishness
- The life-giving power of the Holy Spirit
- The witness of the Holy Spirit
- Our future glory overshadowing our present suffering
- Creation's subjection to the curse
- Our hope for something not yet obtained
- Our inability to pray correctly
- The Holy Spirit's intercession for the saints
- Favorable outcomes

- Foreknowledge, predestination, conformation,[28] and glorification
- Becoming more than a conqueror
- The daily threat of death
- The guarantee of God's love

Considering the multiple topics presented in Romans 1:1 through Romans 8:25, I wondered *in the same way as to what* in the above list does the Holy Spirit help us in our infirmities? I knew that I lacked understanding of this Scripture because all the Scriptures are given by God's divine inspiration (2 Timothy 3:16–17). Thus, I needed the Holy Spirit's help to understand *in like manner to what* does He come to my rescue. I presented myself before God as I studied the book of Romans, especially the eighth chapter: that I might receive discernment to rightly divide the Word of Truth (2 Timothy 2:15). Accordingly, I read and reread different Bible translations.[29] Before and after each reading, I prayed for comprehension of *likewise the Spirit helps*; deep within me, I knew it was a pivotal point the apostle Paul had made.

Hallelujah, God answered my prayer! While going through some old notes, I discovered a photocopy of Romans, the eighth

---

[28] *Conformation* is "to be, or become similar in form, nature, and character," not to be confused with *confirmation*, which means "to establish the truth of."

[29] Advice I received from Larry Huggins is to "let the Bible (different translations) be a commentary to itself." He has at least 150 different Bible translations and paraphrases in his personal library.

chapter, in the *J. B. Phillips New Testament in Modern English.*
The instant I read it illumination flooded my understanding.
I understood that all the topics listed in previous chapters,
mainly the thirty-nine verses of chapter 8, compose one struc-
turally cohesive message of the entire book of Romans. I danced
around my room in glee. For the sake of brevity, I will only
highlight the main points of verses 18–25 of chapter 8 to show
to *what likeness* the Holy Spirit comes to our rescue.

The apostle Paul states that the present hardships in our
lives pale compared to God's future glory for us. Not only do
we look forward to the fulfillment of glorification, but also all
of creation groans in hope for the glorious realization of God's
promises: Creation was made subject to the curse. All creation
was made subject to the curse because Adam disobeyed God;
now it waits for liberation from the tyranny of decay by the
future glory that awaits you and me. Look at verses 19–21 of
Romans chapter 8 in Phillips's translation: *"The whole creation
is on tiptoe to see the wonderful sight of the sons of God coming
into their own. The world of creation cannot as yet see reality, not
because it chooses to be blind, but because in God's purpose it has
been so limited—yet it has been given hope. And the hope is that
in the end the whole of created life will be rescued from the tyranny
of change and decay, and have its share in that magnificent liberty
which can only belong to the children of God!"* (Phillips).

The apostle Paul continues in verse 22 to remind us that
although we are born of the Spirit, we are still human beings
subject to human frailties: *"It is plain to anyone with eyes to*

see that...we who have a foretaste of the Spirit are in a state of painful tension, while we wait for that redemption of our bodies which will mean that at last we have realised[30] our full sonship in him" (vv. 22–23 Phillips). In other words, every child of God yearns for the day when the children of God are no longer subjected to the human frailties that the apostle Paul addressed in Romans 6:1–23 and 7:1–25. Everyone has dealt with or will deal with some form of insecurity. This profound *self*-doubt will cause a person to *self*-sabotage by poor choices, inappropriate behavior, or ill-spoken words. Everyone has had multiple "oh no" moments, which only reinforces existing insecurities in the individual's life. Romans 8:26 sums up in a single word what the apostle Paul described in detail in the preceding sixth and seventh chapters: "infirmities." Other translations and paraphrases render the word *infirmities* as problems, limitations, weaknesses, and inadequacies. In response to emotional, social, physical, or financial demands, too often, we do not make the best choices. Therein lies the cause of our inward groanings.

It is incredible how many preachers and teachers have done their best to explain away those two chapters. They argue that chapters 6 and 7 are referencing a person before salvation. I disagree. The apostle Paul wrote about his personal issues years after his dramatic conversion on the road to Damascus (see Acts 9:1–2). Remember the contention between Paul and Barnabas in Acts 15:36–40. After many successful missionary

---

[30] J. B. Phillips uses the British spelling with an "s" instead of the American spelling with a "z."

trips, the two apostles decided to return to all the regions where they had ministered to see how the churches they had established were progressing. Barnabas wanted to take John Mark with them. Paul disagreed because he was still miffed at John Mark for deserting the two apostles in Pamphylia (Acts 12:25; Acts 13:13). The disagreement over John Mark between the two apostles turned into a heated argument, and the sharp conflict between the two men of God caused their ministry to split. They did not want to work together anymore.

Before we judge Paul and Barnabas or try to diminish the account in Acts 15, let us think about our own experiences after we received salvation. Who among us has not had heated arguments with family, friends, acquaintances, or even strangers? If you have ever engaged in a contentious word-matching conversation, then you have had a heated argument. All of us have succumbed to our personality failings. Who has not experienced blowups at a family gathering? Have you ever made a promise to yourself that you would be lovingly patient with the "it's all about me," drama-seeking family member, but then you failed to keep your promise because that person got on your last nerve? We know all too well the predicament the apostle Paul speaks of in chapter 7: "My own behaviour[31] baffles me. For I find myself not doing what I really want to do but doing what I really loathe....I often find that I have the will to do good, but not the power. That is, I don't accomplish the

---

[31] The Phillips Bible uses the British spelling of *behaviour*—the American spelling is without the "u."

good I set out to do, and the evil [what] I don't really want to do I find I am always doing" (vv. 15–19 Phillips). The apostle Paul states that he has behaved unpleasantly multiple times in his life. Again, after his conversion to Christ, he stated that his behavior baffled him. Before his conversion, he was never perplexed by his actions; he had the blessings of the religious leaders to persecute the early Christians.

Before the apostle Paul's conversion on the road to Damascus, his name was Saul; he had advanced in Judaism beyond many of his contemporaries and was extremely zealous for the traditions of his fathers (Galatians 1:14). He wholeheartedly approved of Stephen's death. He ravaged the early Church, assaulted believers in Christ, and threw both men and women into prison (Acts 8:1, 3 AMP). In Acts 9:1–2, the Bible states that young Saul, still breathing threats and murder against the disciples of the Lord, was relentless in his quest to destroy the early church. So dedicated was he that he asked the high priest for letters of authority giving him the legal right to imprison or kill anyone who believed in Christ. He believed that faith in Christ was heretical; therefore, he believed that the persecution of the church was the will of God. Thus, there was no reason for him to be baffled by his behavior. However, after his conversion to Christ, he realized he needed the help of the Holy Spirit to live a Christian life. Every time he tried to do something without the leading of the Holy Spirit, his behavior disappointed him. The same is true for you and me. I can honestly say that when my behavior was disappointing, it was directly connected to my not following the direction of the Holy Spirit. And before you are tempted to deny your mishandled moments, look at what John the Elder wrote to the churches[32] in Ephesus: *"If we refuse to admit that we [have offended], then we live in a world of illusion and truth becomes a stranger to us. But if we freely admit that we [have offended], we find God utterly reliable . . . he forgives our sins"* (1 John 1:8–9 Phillips).

What John the Elder wrote reminds me of a pastor whom my husband and I met when we lived in Mexico. He was a dear man of God, who has since passed from the earth into glory. The day my husband and I met him and his wife, we knew our hearts were divinely connected. One day he confided in my husband that he was having an extramarital affair. He admitted he knew that it was wrong, but he did not have the will to stop. He loved his wife and was sad that he had broken his marriage vows to her. Not only because of his infidelity was he about to lose his marriage, but also he was going to lose his church and ministry. He asked us to pray with him and for him. We did as he asked.

We prayed for him, his family, and his ministry. It took a while before he ended the affair and reconciled with his wife and family. Later, he shared with us that he would pray in the Spirit every day the entire time he was having an affair. He questioned how he could still have his prayer language during such an ugly

---

[32] Note that John the Elder wrote to the "churches," not to those who had not yet embraced salvation.

time in his life. We explained to him that the Holy Spirit is an ever-present help; the Spirit's purpose is to reconcile our lives to God's plan for our lives. Our pastor friend had been trapped by his emotional and physical desires, but he wanted to be free deep in his heart. It was an agonizing situation for our friend, and he cried out, as the apostle Paul did, *"...who can set me free from the prison of this mortal body? I thank God there is a way out through Jesus Christ our Lord"* (Romans 7:24–25 Phillips).

Again, in Romans 8:22–23, the apostle Paul says that just as all creation is groaning in hope for our future glorification, we, too, are hoping and waiting for the same—the full redemption of our bodies and souls. You and I are not flawless, but we hope in a flawless God to save us. Even in our moments of impatience, disappointment, and failing, we can trust God, the Holy Spirit, to help us. He will boost our hope to obtain the best outcome in every area of life. *"May the God of hope fill you with joy and peace in your faith, that by the power of the Holy Spirit, your whole life and outlook may be radiant with hope"* (Romans 15:13 Phillips). God wants our perspective, our attitude toward life, to be glowing with hope—*expectation*, which is the strong belief that God hears and answers our prayers.

The Holy Spirit helps you and me hold fast to our confidence in the immutable promise of God's glory. He floods our hearts with expectation as we wait with patience for the realization of God's glory in every situation in our lives—even if we are at fault. You and I will have issues in life that will be impossible for us to resolve on our own: it is a fact of life.[33] Yet, with God on our side, all things are possible.[34] God's glory is to help us live a victorious life, even when our behavior is disappointing. Christ died to pay for our past, present, and future offenses. At the request of Christ, God sent the Holy Spirit to be our ever-present Helper. And, *likewise,* the Holy Spirit comes to our rescue, to help us in our present limitations, even when we blow it, because He is the Spirit of Hope.

~~~

Likewise, this changes everything!

---

[33] In Luke 17:1, Jesus said, "Betrayals are inevitable" (TPT).

[34] See these additional Scriptures: Matthew 17:20; 19:26; Mark 10:27; Luke 1:37; 18:27.

3

Help!

The Spirit also helpeth our infirmities.

—Romans 8:26

*I*n the New Testament Greek, the word *helpeth* is a three-part compound word: *sunantilambano*. To better understand the meaning of that Greek word, I will dissect it into its three parts: a) *sun*, meaning "together with"; b) *anti*, meaning "over against"; and c) *lambano*, meaning "to take." This word describes the helper's action. The *helper* is to aid the person in need of assistance to obtain the desired results by cooperating or striving with that person. For example, several years ago, I helped one of my sisters do a makeover of her fourth-floor one-bedroom apartment. She had a 1950s modern office desk in her bedroom. It was a monstrous piece of furniture, at least 5 feet wide, almost 3 feet tall, and about 4 feet deep. My sister was trying to handle this piece of furniture by herself. The more she tried to remove the desk from her bedroom, the more it became wedged in her bedroom door. She needed my help. There was no way I was going to take over the task for my sister, who was in her mid-fifties, as I had just celebrated my seventieth birthday. What I did was come to her aid to assist her in accomplishing the desired result, removing the desk from her apartment. Together we lifted, twisted, pulled, and dragged the desk out of her apartment to the street-level recycling area on the opposite side of her apartment building. Again, I did not take over her task; I simply aided her in finishing the job. An aide does not take over the person's responsibility but assists that person in accomplishing the desired results. A biblical example is given in Luke 10:40, when Martha said to Jesus concerning her sister, Mary: "Lord . . . bid her therefore that she help me." Martha used the Greek word *sunantilambano.*

Many Bible teachers have a negative view of Martha based on Jesus' response to her: "Oh Martha, Martha, you are so anxious and concerned about a million details, but really, only one thing matters. Mary has chosen that one thing, and I won't take it away from her" (Luke 10:41–42 Voice). Before we join the ranks of Martha's critics, let us examine the backstory that led to her mini-meltdown. In the first verse of Luke 10, Jesus has recruited and ordained seventy disciples (in addition to the original twelve) to go ahead of Him, in teams of two, to every town He planned to visit. The newly ordained disciples served as delegates for Jesus' traveling ministry. As forerunners, they went to the places that Jesus designated and announced to the people that Jesus was coming to their towns. Their assignment was the same as that of John the Baptist, the forerunner of Christ: *"John cried out, 'Look! There he is . . . I told you that a Mighty One would come who is far greater than I am!"* (John 1:29–30 TPT).

Jesus instructed the seventy disciples to pray that God would send out more workers to win souls for God. He warned them that what He commissioned them to do would not be an easy task. He ordered them not to take any provisions with them, that they were to trust God for their well-being. He admonished them not to get distracted from His purpose. Finally, He told them to seek out a house[35] when they arrived in a town, and if the owner of the house was hospitable, then they should speak peace to that family. After several more instructions to the newly ordained disciples, Jesus concludes with these words, "Remember . . . Whoever listens to your message is actually listening to me" (TPT).[36]

During his forty-plus years of ministry, my husband, Larry Huggins, held numerous crusades in the United States of America (USA) and around the world. Just as Jesus did in Luke

---

[35] *Strong's* definition renders the word house as "property, wealth, goods."
[36] Read Luke 10:1–12.

10:1–16, Larry Huggins sent representatives of his ministry to places where he planned to minister. Their job was to represent his ministry and generate support from the local churches, local officials, and the local media before he arrived to hold the crusades. He often planned to minister in places where no one knew him or his ministry. I am reminded of when the Holy Spirit led him to hold a crusade in Leon, Mexico. As far as Larry knew, he did not know anyone in Leon, nor did anyone in that city know him. Larry met a young man who lived in Fresno, California, by the Holy Spirit's direction. After receiving the charge, the young man went to Leon, Mexico, as Larry's representative. God's hand was upon that young man.[37] He met with twenty or more local pastors, officials, and members of the media, gaining their support for the upcoming crusade, to be held within two weeks. My husband traveled to Leon a few weeks later to meet the pastors, wives, and associate ministers. He ministered to them as they enjoyed the luncheon he provided. It was a successful gathering, and I was thankful that the luncheon was catered. It is quite possible that I would have had a mini-meltdown, as did Martha, if I had had to prepare a meal for forty-plus guests!

Again, in Luke 10:1, Jesus commissioned seventy disciples to go ahead of Him into every town that He planned to visit. Remember, He had instructed the seventy to search out a family,

[37] For Larry Huggins' detailed account of this miraculous direction of God, follow this link: https://zchurch.life/2021/04/01/the-holy-spirit-helps-us-do-big-things-for-god-by-larry-huggins/.

and if the family was hospitable, they were to stay with that family. According to Jesus' instructions, they were to become a part of the hosting family. That is something to think about. Imagine several strangers arriving at your home, and no one had warned you that they were coming. After a few moments of pleasantries, they inform you that they represent *so-and-so's* ministry and require of you your unlimited hospitality. In response to the puzzled look on your face, they also tell you they require three cooked meals per day, a clean and furnished bedroom, and uncontested control of the television remote control because, as a representative of *so-and-so's* ministry, they are to be accepted as members of your family. How would you respond to such demands from strangers? Would you consent to their requests? Well, that is the scenario in which Martha found herself. (Of course, minus the remote control.)

Skipping down to verses 38 and 39 of Luke 10, we learn that Jesus and His disciples traveled to a village where Martha lived. She welcomed the Lord and His ministry team into her home. It is not clear how many disciples came with Jesus in addition to the twelve disciples: it was Jesus' entire traveling ministry team. You can easily empathize with Martha if you imagine that at least thirteen hungry men—maybe more—have arrived at your home, and you are obliged[38] to be hospitable. Please note that *hospitality* is one of the gifts of the Spirit mentioned in Romans 12:6 and 12:13:

---

[38] *Obliged* means "bound by duty, ethics, or politeness."

God's marvelous grace imparts to each one of us varying gifts . . . [and ministries that are uniquely ours, such as, to] eagerly welcome people as guests into your home (TPT).

Martha was anxious about the accommodation for her guests. I identify with Martha because I, too, have prepared sit-down dinners for ten or more guests. Dinner-party preparations can be quite demanding, which includes creating a guest list, menu planning, tableware choice, table setting, decoration and atmosphere preparation, background music, guests' gift, in addition to the preparation of the food itself, and much more.

Regardless of how well-planned my events are, there always seems to be a last-minute issue. For example, the signature dessert looks nothing like the photo in the recipe book. Or I left myself too little time to dress before my guests are to arrive. In overwhelming moments like those, I ask my husband to help. He always comes to my aid, which allows me time to recenter my thoughts. It is paramount for a host/hostess to be poised before guests arrive. If the hosts are frazzled when the guests arrive, it only makes for awkward moments. To loosely quote the inventor of modern baroque, Dorothy Draper (1889-1969),[39] *"You aim at the heart when you give your guests joy, gaiety, and excitement."* Once, my husband's buddy invited us to his home for dinner, and we accepted. Unbeknownst to us,

---

[39] Dorothy Draper was aptly proclaimed "America's most fabulous decorator." For more information, visit https://www.dorothydraper.com/history/.

he had not consulted with his wife. We became aware of his faux pas after we arrived because the wife stayed in her upstairs bedroom for more than a half hour before she decided to finally acknowledge us, making for an uncomfortable evening.

It is worth repeating: The gift of hospitality is listed with the other gifts of the Spirit, including prophecy, teaching, and generosity, to name a few (see Romans 12:6–13). Martha had the gift of hospitality. To quote Oprah Winfrey,[40] *"One of life's great compliments . . . [its] pleasure . . . is that of literally welcoming people into your space, letting people in."* Martha, not Mary, opened her home to Jesus and His disciples.[41] Nevertheless, she became overwhelmed and cried out for help while doing what she enjoyed most. Her plea for help was not unreasonable. Martha did not want Mary to take over the meal preparations. All Martha wanted was some assistance from Mary. I did not want my husband to take over my dinner-party preparations when I asked for his help. Nor did I want to move the desk from my sister's apartment by myself. *Likewise, the Spirit* {sunantilambano} *helpeth*—that is, the Holy Spirit comes to give us support to live our best lives. He cooperates with us in our endeavors, and we are to cooperate with Him as He assists us.

---

[40] For more about Oprah Winfrey, visit https://www.biography.com/media-%0Dfigure/oprah-winfrey#:~:text=Oprah%20Winfrey%20is%20a%20talk, Oprah%0D%20Winfrey%20Network%20(OWN

[41] Luke 10:38 says this: "Now it came to pass…a certain woman named Martha received [Jesus and disciples] into her house."

Everyone has felt stressed due to life's demands and challenges from time to time and has cried out for help. When Jesus said, "I will pray the Father [to] give you another Comforter" (John 14:16), He used the Greek word *parakletos*. He said that He would ask the Father to send you and me a Helper who would aid, assist, and support us in our endeavors to live an abundant life. Jesus taught that we are to persist in our pleas for help in His parable about the widow and the unjust judge. He started the parable in Luke 18:1–8 with these words: *"That men ought always to pray, and not to faint."* In the example, Jesus described an officer of the court as a wicked judge with no respect for God or humanity.

Also, in this story, a widow sought the judge's help against her ruthless adversaries. Each day the widow begged the unjust judge to help her. Each day he refused to acknowledge her pleas. But she did not give up: She was relentless. Regardless of how hopeless a situation may seem, we must remain persistent in our prayers for help. In the end, because of the widow's importunity, the unjust judge gave in to her pleas and ruled in her favor. Jesus ended the parable with a question: *"Did you hear what the godless judge said—that he would answer her persistent request?"* (Luke 18:6 TPT). His question focuses on the stark contrast between the unjust judge and a just God. To explain, if a wicked judge responds to the widow's need, how much more will our loving heavenly Father respond to our persistent pleas for help? Jesus assured us that God will answer us. He will flood our lives with the help of the Holy Spirit.

The widow did not want the wicked judge to live her life. She wanted his help. The apostle Paul, in his many prayers for the saints,[42] never once prayed that the Holy Spirit would exempt a saint of his or her responsibilities to live victoriously. He prayed that the saint would receive help to live a victorious life. The indwelling Spirit is an ever-present Helper who aids us in all areas of our lives. He does not take over our responsibility to fulfill the purpose of our lives; instead, He helps us to live our best lives.

The Holy Spirit's help changes everything!

---

[42] For Holy Spirit-inspired prayers, see: Ephesians 1:18–21; 3:17–21; Philippians 1:9–11; and Colossians 1:9–20.

4

The Purpose of the Holy Spirit

And he who searches our hearts knows the mind of the Spirit, because the Spirit intercedes for God's people in accordance with the will of God.

—ROMANS 8:27 NIV

*W*hat is the *mind* of the Spirit? In our modern definition of the word *mind*, we understand it to mean "the totality of conscious: reason, thought, feeling, and perception."[43] However, the word *mind* in Romans 8:27 is the Greek word *phronema*,

---

[43] Dictionary.com digital dictionary

which implies *purpose*.[44] Now, the word *purpose* can be a noun, or it can be a verb, depending on how it is used in speech, and however it is used, its meaning remains unchanged[45]:

- ❧ As a noun: the reason for which something exists, or is done, made, used—<u>determination</u>: <u>resoluteness</u>.

- ❧ As a verb: to set as an aim, intention, or goal, <u>to resolve to do something</u>.

The Holy Spirit is resolved to help you and me enjoy victorious living in Christ; therefore, an essential part of His ministry in our lives is to help you and me to pray in harmony with God's will for our respective lives, because "God (has) prepared [for us] . . . [the good life]" (Ephesians 2:10 AMP).

Although God's plan is unique for each person, there is the primary will of God for humanity. Before you or I can enjoy God's specific plan for our individual lives, we must understand and embrace God's basic will for all our lives. I am reminded of the lesson I learned in grade school about the importance of the *basics* in everything we do in life. During the home economics period, my classmates and I were delighted to learn that our class project was *cake-baking*. We were divided into groups of

---

[44] *Strong's Concordance* #G5427 transliterated the word *phronema*, from #G5426; "(mental) inclination or **purpose**." *Thayer's* definition is "what one has in the mind, the thoughts, and purposes." (Also, see footnotes 5 and 6 for information on *Strong's* and *Thayer's*.)

[45] Definition taken from iPhone App Dictionary.com (©2018 Dictionary.com, LLC).

four. Each group was instructed to decide on a type of cake to make. The classroom was abuzz with excited chatter as each group made plans for the cake project. At the end of the class period, we turned in our cake designs to the teacher.

The following day, we returned to home economics and were delightfully surprised to see that the teacher had set up a cooking station. Yet, we were somewhat confused that there was only one cooking station. We wondered if the eight groups of four would have to share the lone station; we reasoned that the teacher would pick the group with the best design to be the first to use the cooking station. While we waited for class to begin, we laughingly bantered each other about whose cake choice was the best. We were having fun, and then the bell rang. The teacher cleared her throat. We knew what that meant. All chatter stopped. We took our assigned seats and waited for her instructions. She said that she was pleased with all our choices; however, it would be two weeks before we would start on our chosen cake designs. In unison, we groaned in protest. The teacher allowed us to express our disappointment for about a minute.

She explained that before a person could become a creative baker—as we all thought we were—that person needed to learn and develop basic baking skills. Once again, we groaned at her words, especially at the word *basic* because, to a group of eleven-year-olds, the word *basic* was synonymous with the word *boring*. Not one bit was the teacher phased by our groans. First, she explained the setup of the cooking station and the different cooking tools. Then she explained the different ingredients on display, which were needed to make a basic cake. Finally, she explained the importance of organization, attention to detail, understanding culinary terms, converting measurements, food temperature, and handling different types of food—such as cracking an egg and sifting flour. She stressed that in addition to developing our cooking skills, we needed the skill of patience. She assured us that many of our cooking creations would only be suitable for the trash can; however, she encouraged us not to lose patience with ourselves because if we continued to learn, we would eventually prepare beautiful meals for others to enjoy. I can attest that she was right, because six decades later, I still have cooking failures, and always nearby is my trusty trash can. I am grateful for the lesson I learned in grade school about the importance of the *basics*.

There are basics of God's will for each person's life. Those basics—that is, the essential principles of life—do not vary from person to person: rich or poor, married or single, male or female, educated or uneducated, or whatever other demographics used. God's primary will is the same for everyone—no variants. Let us look at a few Scriptures as examples of God's *basic* will for everyone[46]:

- ◦ God wants us to live a pure life, free of sexual immorality; to learn how to control our bodily desires; to not

---

[46] Please note that the following Scriptures have been loosely quoted.

violate or take advantage of others. We are to seek holiness. (See 1 Thessalonians 4:3–8 Voice.)

Are there any demographics that should be exempted from the above basic will of God? Even children should be taught that violation of self and others is wrong at an early age.

Here is the next example:

- God wants us to show appreciation to those who care for our spiritual well-being; to encourage one another; to be quick to be patient with others; to resist the urge of vengeance; to have a heart of gratitude; to live a life of prayer . . . for this is God's perfect plan for us in Christ Jesus. (See 1 Thessalonians 5:12–18 Voice.)

To ask the same question again: Are there any demographics that should be excluded from obeying this aspect of God's basic will? No group of people—neither has there ever been, nor will there ever be—is excused from being kind and patient with others, showing appreciation to others, and never seeking vengeance on others. That is just the primary way to live in this world.

Here is another example from Scripture:

- In our prayer life we are to pray for all men, which includes every political leader and representative, because God longs for everyone to embrace His life and know the full knowledge of truth. (See 1 Timothy 2:1–4 TPT.).

Is there any demographic of born-again believers who are excused from "imitating God as a dear child"?[47] In other words, how can a person imitate God as a dear child if that person condemns others who have a differing opinion to hell? The Bible tells us that the Lord God reveals His loving patience toward all because He does not want anyone to perish; what God wants is for all to come to repentance (see 2 Peter 3:9).

Even Jesus in His human form had to learn the basics of God's will for His life on earth:

> In the days of his flesh, Jesus offered up prayers and supplications with loud cries and tears, to him who was able to save him from death, and he was heard for his godly fear. Although he was a Son, he learned obedience through what he suffered.
>
> —HEBREWS 5:7–8 RSV

Now that we know the basics of God's will, how should we advance to the specifics of God's will for our respective lives? Therein lies the Holy Spirit's purpose, that is, to help us progress in the specifics of our lives. His purpose is to enable us to pray in *"perfect harmony with God's plan."*[48] How does He help us? The Spirit reconciles our prayers—our desires, wants, hopes, and fears—to God's will as our guide into all truth.

---

[47] "Be imitators of God in everything you do, for then you will represent your Father as his beloved sons and daughters" (Ephesians 5:1 TPT).

[48] See Romans 8:27 TPT.

Let us look at the word *reconciling* in terms of balancing your monthly bank statement. The word *reconcile* is from the old French words *re* and *conciliare*, which mean "to bring together" and "back"; in other words, "to make *friendly*, again." To accurately reconcile your bank balance with your book balance, you need a list of all banking activities made during a given month, including any outstanding transactions not included in the bank statement. For example, consider receiving your bank statement, and it shows that you have a balance of $1,000; however, minutes before you read your bank statement, you made an online purchase of $300. Your actual balance is reduced to $700, despite what your bank statement shows. You must adjust your banking records to agree with your bank and book balances. If you do not, you will have money problems; for example, you could spend money you do not have.

Interestingly, Romans 8:7 states that *"the carnal mind is enmity against God"*; the same Greek word for mind in this verse is the same Greek word found in Romans 8:27: *"he . . . knows the mind of the Spirit."* The word carnal in verse 7 refers to the human nature and its passions; therefore, Romans 8:7 can be read as follows: *The purpose of the human nature is always at odds with God's will.* Our human nature is our dispositions and characteristics: the way we think, feel, act, and react. The Spirit of Truth's intent is to change our tendencies to be friendly to God's plan; that is His purpose. It has been said that there can be three or more opinions between two people because each person is motivated by their own personal feelings and beliefs.

Two persons living together can have opposing views. For example, my husband is a true Texan. He enjoys all types of foods—especially a prime cut of beef. I am just the opposite. Over forty years ago, I eliminated beef, pork, and crustaceans from my diet because I believe those foods are unhealthy. You may think, *So what? You and your husband have different eating habits.* Those differences have made for some interesting family discussions.

Even at a church service where one would think everyone in attendance agrees with one another; yet, that is not reality because people vary in their reasons for attending church services. Repeatedly, history has proven that Christians will split a church, get divorced, end friendships, even slander one another based on differences of opinion. Church people have fought over such silly issues as church decorations, types of seats, seating arrangements, and more. For example, one church in central Texas commissioned a company to design and install a water fountain to enhance the entrance into the church building. Years after the installation of the fountain, the pastor's wife griped to anyone who would listen. Her husband, the church pastor, liked the water fountain installation. Their differences of opinion often led to heated words just as the church service was about to begin. Each time my husband and I were their guests and witnessed their difference of opinion over the fountain, it was awkward and embarrassing for us.

If two or more people are in conflict (as were the pastor and his wife in central Texas, or as were Paul and Barnabas in Acts

15), is God obligated to choose a side based on who is His favorite? Does God choose to listen to one person and reject the other person? I do not believe that is the case. I think the person who willingly yields to the Holy Spirit's ministry will see the goodness of God. If everyone involved in the scrimmage decides to yield to the Spirit, everyone will see God's goodness. The goodness of God can bring a dramatic change of heart, including the realization that a situation is being mishandled; thus, all may experience the reconciling power of the Holy Spirit.

We need the Spirit's help to not give in to our strong emotions, preconceived notions, and limited knowledge, which are, most of the time, at odds with God's will for us, our family, our friends, and the world. It is important to note that even though our wishes and wants, at times, are at odds with God's plan for us, this is not always because we are willfully rebelling against God. It can be a matter of self-preservation: right or wrong. Too often, we are blinded by our personal beliefs, desires, and feelings; therefore, our ability to discern the truth is limited.

During those times, we rehearsed the problem or relived the injustice while trying to pray that God's will is done. We want answers. We want change. We want retribution. We want help. The Holy Spirit is keenly aware of our hearts' desires, and He is committed to helping us.

The Holy Spirit's purpose is to make our prayers, which are filled with our emotions, harmonize with the will and plan of

God for our lives. Remember that to *reconcile* is to make one's account consistent with another by considering all transactions, including those that have begun but are not yet completed. When you and I pray, the Spirit scrutinizes every detail of our lives—past, present, and future—as He makes our requests compatible with God's will. During the reading of this book, you may be dealing with situations that have existed for years—"an outstanding balance," figuratively. Please take courage, because He who has begun a good work in you—in your life—will complete it all.[49]

The Holy Spirit knows what we are made of—dust.[50] He knows that we, both male and female, are emotional beings: We are passionate about our likes and dislikes. He knows that we deal with all types of issues every day—big and small. At times, things may seem unbearable, so much so that we may even identify with Job[51]. The demand to make a good decision can be daunting during those times. Our hearts' cry is to make good choices—we want a better life for ourselves and our loved ones.

The Spirit of God knows our hearts' yearnings better than we do. Also, the Spirit knows the price Christ Jesus paid so that

---

[49] See Philippians 1:6 and Psalm 138:8.
[50] See Psalm 103:13–14.
[51] According to the book of Job, in one day, Job loses all his wealth, and his ten children are killed by a storm. Job is afflicted with horrible skin sores. His wife demands that he curse God and die. See https://www.sparknotes.com/lit/oldtestament/section11/#:~:text=Important%20Quotations%20Explained-,Summary,appears%20before%20God%20in%20heaven.

we could have abundant life. Jesus said, "I came to give life with joy and abundance" (John 10:10 Voice). We are born of God to fulfill the destiny He has given each of us. Thus, the *purpose* of the Holy Spirit is to reconcile, that is, to bring our hearts' desires—concerning all issues of life—into complete agreement with God's will for our lives.

~~~~~

The Holy Spirit's purpose changes everything!

5

He Who Searches Our Hearts

God, the searcher of the heart, knows fully our longings, yet he also understands the desires of the Spirit, because the Holy Spirit passionately pleads before God for us...in perfect harmony with God's plan and our destiny.

—ROMANS 8:27 TPT

*T*his Scripture passage implies that you and I have the "triune God[52] in council, convened during our times of prayer"

---

[52] The triune God consists of God the Father; God the Son; and God the Holy Spirit—these three comprise the Godhead.

43

(Wuest): This would be an appropriate time to use the word *awesome!*[53] The phrase *"God the searcher of the heart"* is a picture of God the Almighty carefully and systematically examining every detail, fact, and even allegation of our thoughts. Let us ponder on this truth, that God, Christ, and the Holy Spirit intimately know each one of us. Christ Jesus ultimately identified with us, not as a group, but as individuals. He lived every moment of your life as if yours were the only life to live. He did the same for me. His blood poured from His veins for each of us. Christ sees the world through your eyes because on the cross He identified with you. Yet on the cross He also identified with me: He sees the world filtered through my perception of life. Christ identified with every single person who has ever lived on this earth. He has experienced every nuance of our emotions— the good and the not-so-good. By His blood, He reconciled everything in your life, in my life, and in everyone else's life to God's will. *Everyone?* you may ask. Yes, *everyone!* Again, 2 Peter 3:9 states that God does not want anyone to perish. According to the Population Reference Bureau (PRB),[54] about 117 billion[55] people from the beginning of time until the writing of this book have been born on the earth.

---

[53] The word *awesome* has been overused and misused by popular culture; however, the word means *"inducing awe; inspiring an overwhelming feeling of reverence, admiration, or fear."*

[54] To learn more about Population Reference Bureau (PRB), visit its website at https://www.prb.org/.

[55] The number 117 billion written in Arabic numerals is 117,000,000,000.

Jesus Christ had to live 117 billion–plus lives (including those of the unborn) to cover everyone with His redeeming blood; that means that He, Christ the Savior, is intimately acquainted with you, me, and everyone else. He knows our thoughts. Medical experts estimate that the human mind has between fifty thousand and eighty thousand thoughts per day. Now, multiply 117 billion people times fifty thousand thoughts per day, and that times 365 days per year, and that times an average lifespan: The figure is astronomical! Yet not one of our thoughts goes unexamined by God, because Jesus, our High Priest, is absolutely in touch with our reality (see Hebrews 4:14–16 MSG). Our hearts' secrets are intimately known by God, Christ, and our Helper, the Holy Spirit.

Lord, you know everything there is to know about me. You perceive every movement of my heart and soul, and you understand my every thought before it even enters my mind.

—PSALM 139:1–2 TPT

The Holy Spirit is ever-present to help us (Romans 8:26). Let us face the fact that our thoughts often get us into awkward situations because as we think, we act. How often have we acted or reacted inappropriately based on our thoughts and feelings? On the other hand, who has not been duped by a duplicitous person pretending to be a friend? (See Proverbs 23:6–8.) That is why we need the help of God's Spirit, not only to penetrate the deepest parts of our being, but also to penetrate the deepest parts of everyone else's being.

Not all situations are sinister when it comes to individuals having conflicting thoughts. Here is a comical example. Throughout my thirty-plus years of marriage to Larry, I have looked to him to capture and kill all spiders within twenty feet of me. My reaction to spiders is always the same, regardless of size, which is a bloodcurdling scream. Without fail, Larry comes to my rescue. Finally, one day he confessed to me that he had a deep-seated aversion to spiders. I had no idea! He always exhibited a calm demeanor. How was I to know that he was mentally freaking out each time he encountered a spider? This is proof that we do not always know what another person is thinking.

Numerous scientific studies have proven that even though people have co-experienced an event, their perception of the event widely varies. As the Scripture states, *"Who can see into a man's heart and know his thoughts?"*[56] God, the Searcher of hearts, knows all: *"Everyone and everything is exposed, opened for His inspection."*[57] To repeat, you and I, on the average, have at least fifty thousand thoughts per day, and not one goes unnoticed by the Holy Spirit. When you and I pray in the Spirit, we have a decisive advantage, because the triune God, the most significant and most potent council ever to convene, intervenes on our behalf. Nothing is hidden from this powerful Council.

---

[56] See 1 Corinthians 2:11 Voice.

[57] See Hebrews 4:13 Voice.

The amazing summary of this chapter is this: It does not matter how out of sorts our hearts' secrets, thoughts, and feelings are toward God; if we yield to the Holy Spirit, He will always help us to pray according to the divine purpose of God for our lives and for the lives of others.

The Searcher of the heart's secrets
changes everything!

6

The Perfect Will of God

But He Who searches men's hearts needs no words to learn what occupies the mind of the Spirit: He knows that [the Spirit's] intercessions on behalf of God's Hallowed People are in harmony with the Divine Will.

—ROMANS 8:27 WADE

It is essential to address the subject of the *will* of *God* by looking at Romans 12:2: "Be transformed...by the renewing of your mind...so that you may prove [for yourselves] what the will of God is, that which is good and acceptable and perfect [in His plan and purpose for you]" (AMP). This Scripture has not been discerned correctly[58] by many Bible teachers. Thus, it has not been taught correctly. Consequently, many people believe that God has three different wills for everyone. Such erroneous teaching!

In 1963, an American television game show, *Let's Make a Deal*,[59] aired on the National Broadcasting Company (NBC).[60] The format of this daytime television show required the show's host to select members from the studio audience and make deals with them. The host would give the contestant something of value—for example, two thousand dollars in cash; then the host would offer the contestant an exchange of the cash for one of three mystery gifts. If the participant chose to trade, three doors were presented, but the secret item behind the door was not revealed until the participant selected a door. Sometimes the door chosen would reveal an all-expenses-paid vacation, a new set of furniture, a new car—and much more. At other times, the door chosen would reveal a dismal, valueless item called *zonks*. For example, some of the game show *zonks* were junk cars, old wheelbarrows, giant teddy bears, and hugely oversized articles of clothing: All were of no value to the contestant. It was always a gamble because the contestant never knew what to expect,

---

[58] See 2 Timothy 2:15.

[59] To learn more about this game show, visit https://en.wikipedia.org/wiki/Let%27s_Make_a_Deal.

[60] The National Broadcasting Company (NBC) is an American television network.

although they were hoping for the best. Often, the contestants were miserably disappointed in their choices.

Sadly, many Bible teachers have taught Romans 12:2 as if it follows the same structure of the *Let's Make a Deal* television show; based on life choices, a person will end up in one of the three "wills" of God. My husband and I have acquaintances who have argued to the point of frustration that God's will is comprised of three levels. The King James rendering of Romans 12:2 fosters the idea that there are three "wills" of God: "what is that good, and acceptable, and perfect, will of God." Thus, the belief that God has three "wills" involves these options:

- Choose "Door Number One": the *good will* of God.
- Choose "Door Number Two": the *acceptable* will of God.
- Choose "Door Number Three": the *perfect* will of God.

The erroneous belief in the "three wills" of God can be explained as follows:

1. The *good will* of God takes place when you are *not quite* doing what God wants in your life. At least what you are doing is satisfactory or adequate, and so God is okay with your modification of His plan for your life.

2. Next is the *acceptable will* of God. You are *slightly more* yielded to God at this level than you would be in the first level; however, you still modify God's plan for your life by making as many tweaks as necessary to suit your desires. God accepts the tweaks you have made to His

will. His attitude is, *If you're okay with it, then I'm okay with it.* Hence, the *acceptable will* of God.

3. Finally, we come to the jackpot of all God's "wills." Drumroll, please. *Ta-da!* The *perfect will* of God is the *highest* of the "three wills," which only enlightened people achieve. If you can attain this level, all your dreams come true.

Too many dear souls (including me) have lived under the condemnation of not being in God's "perfect will," and we believe this because we still face financial struggles, personal setbacks, physical limitations, or all the above. This unfounded teaching has been propagated for much too long: More than once, a well-known preacher or evangelist has said that people are not wealthy because "God cannot trust them with money." (I'm guessing the bulk of Christendom has picked the wrong door.) Here is a thought to ponder: Imagine God's surprise when He found out that Adam and Eve could not be trusted after He had given them rulership over all His creation. No one has ever been as wealthy as Adam and Eve were in the beginning. They had the entire planet earth to themselves—and then they blew it. This unfounded teaching of the different levels of God's will has caused many people to live defeated lives.

Each day, as the struggles of life persist, condemnation screams, "YOU MUST NOT BE IN GOD'S WILL!" Other condemning thoughts flood our minds, such as, *If you were in God's will for your life, then you would not have these problems.* Or, *What sin in your past is keeping you from presently enjoying life?* I know this pain of condemnation because for many years, I cried out to God, begging Him to at least give me a clue why I was not as wealthy as all the so-and-sos I knew. I fasted and prayed. Repeatedly, I begged for forgiveness for any offenses real or imagined. Then one day, I realized that Christ died for me, and that the only will of God for me is to believe in the *substitution work* of Christ. He paid for all my faults and nailed those offenses to the cross. There is, therefore, no condemnation to me because I am in Christ, and His Spirit of Life has made me free from the law of condemnation—the law of death!

Again, "the three wills of God" is an erroneous teaching that may have its roots in Gnosticism.[61] God has only *one specific will* for your life.[62] You may find yourself taking different approaches to His plan for your life, but His plan does not change. God only has one plan for you, that is, "to prosper you, not to harm you . . . to give you a future filled with hope (Jeremiah 29:11 NET). The words *good, acceptable,* and *perfect* are adjectives that modify the phrase *will of God.* Let us look at different translations of Romans 12:2, including the King James Version:

---

[61] Gnosticism was a prominent heretical movement of the second-century Christian Church, partly of pre-Christian origin. Gnostic doctrine taught that the world was created and ruled by a lesser divinity, the demiurge, and that Christ was an emissary of the remote supreme divine being, esoteric knowledge (gnosis), of whom enabled the redemption of the human spirit; see https://www.britannica.com/topic/gnosticism.

[62] Please reference chapter 4 of this book, titled *The Purpose of the Holy Spirit,* to understand the writer's distinction between God's basic will for all humanity and God's specific will for each individual discussed in this chapter.

- "by the renewal of your mind…you may discern what is the will of God, what is good and[63] acceptable and perfect" (ESV).

- "you will be able to test and approve what God's will is—his good, pleasing and perfect will" (NIV).

- "be ye reformed in newness of your wit, that ye prove … the will of God, good, and well-pleasing, and perfect" (Wycliffe).

- "be ye transformed by the renewing of your mind, that ye may prove what is that good, and acceptable, and perfect, will of God" (KJV).

- "let God re-make you so that your whole attitude of mind is changed. Thus, you will prove in practice that the will of God is good, acceptable…and perfect" (Phillips).

- "let your behaviour change, modelled by your new mind. This is the only way to discover the will of God and know what is good, what it is that God wants, what is the perfect thing to do" (TJB).

Note that in each translation, including the King James Version, the word *will* is singular and not plural. None of the translations read *the good, or the pleasing, or the perfect wills of God*. You and I are to yield ourselves to the ministry of the

---

[63] Note the usage of the conjunction *and*—used to connect words that are to be taken jointly, and not the usage of the conjunction *or*—which is used to link alternatives, for example, "a cup of tea or coffee."

Holy Spirit so that a renewal, renovation, and complete change for the better in our mental process and emotional attitude will happen. We will, then, discover that God's specific plan for our respective lives meets all the specifications of our hearts' desires (Wuest). Yielding to the Holy Spirit, we will learn that:

- God's plan is good—possessing all the qualities required for a *good life.*

- God's plan is well-pleasing—satisfying every area of our lives.

- God's plan is perfect—giving us victory in all issues of our lives.

- To the greatest extent or degree, God's plan is complete— producing all that is needed to fulfill our hearts' desires.

Yielding to God's good, well-pleasing, and perfect will for you—*how is that a bad plan?*[64]

God's perfect, good, and satisfying will
changes everything!

---

[64] This is a quote by Jacopo, a character in the movie *The Count of Monte Cristo.*

7

We Just Do Not Know

Likewise the Spirit also helpeth our infirmities: for we know not what we should pray for as we ought: but the Spirit [Himself] maketh intercession for us with groanings which cannot be uttered.

—ROMANS 8:26

The Living Bible renders the above Scripture in these words: "The Holy Spirit helps us with our daily problems and in our praying. For we don't even know what we should pray for nor how to pray as we should."

Before I knew the words of Romans 8:26–27 (even as a young child), I prayed to God, and many of my prayers were answered. Perhaps you have had the same experience as I had. We must have done something right to enjoy answered prayers. (That seems like a valid argument, right?) Maybe you were taught to pray Sidney Mitchell's 1920 *Children's Prayer:* "Now I lay me down to sleep. I pray the Lord my soul to keep. If I should die before I wake, I pray the Lord my soul to take."[65] Assuming that prayer worked, you woke up the next morning. Frankly, I never liked that prayer, especially the part about dying before waking up. Thankfully, my mother taught me to recite the Lord's Prayer before I went to bed, which is a far better example of how to pray than Mitchell's dark-themed nursery rhyme.

In Matthew 6:9–13 and Luke 11:2–4, we find Jesus' guidelines to how to pray the Lord's Prayer:[66]

- ❧ We acknowledge God as our Father.
- ❧ We bless and honor His name.
- ❧ We ask for the presence of the Spirit.
- ❧ We ask that God's will be done on earth, as it is done in heaven.
- ❧ We ask for portions for our daily lives.

---

[65] "Now I Lay Me Down to Sleep," lyrics by Sidney D. Mitchell; music by George W. Meyer, 1920.

[66] Some Bible teachers are of the thought that the "Lord's Prayer" is a misnomer because Luke 11:2–4 is Jesus' response to the disciples' request to teach them how to pray (Luke 11:1).

- We ask for forgiveness for our offenses.

- We extend forgiveness to others for their offenses.

- We ask for guidance and deliverance.

- We acknowledge the total rulership, inherent power, and glorious dignity of God.

- We end the prayer with *Amen.*

Jesus' instructions are straightforward and easy to follow. Plus, we have the apostle Paul's prayers throughout his epistles as examples of how to pray.[67] Nonetheless, Romans 8:26 states that you and I do not know *how* to pray as we should, which seems to be a contradiction, considering all the instructions and examples of prayer that are given in the Bible.

The word "infirmities" in the New Testament Greek is *astheneia*: It means "frailty, feebleness, weakness, lack of strength, or lack of the capacity to do what is necessary." Infirmities in this passage of Scripture are not physical, but spiritual in the context of prayer. In other words, our weakness is our inability to know *what* to pray. We may know the general problem, and whatever the problem may be, we know to go to God in prayer. Yet what we do not know are the specifics of that problem.[68] Our prayers' objectives are clear: We want God to help us "quick, fast, and right away." But do we know the particulars of any given

---

[67] Here are a few Scripture references with prayers of the apostle Paul: Ephesians 1:17–23; 3:14–21; Philippians 1:4–11; Colossians 1:9–17; 1 Thessalonians 5:23.

[68] Wuest Greek New Testament.

situation? No, we do not. During such challenging times, we are often blindsided by the bombardment of feelings, speculations, hopes, fears, and impulses, which impairs our ability to make good choices.

Every day we are inundated with all types of threats. At the time of this writing, the world is dealing with the mutations of the COVID-19 virus. In addition to the virus threats, there are hotspots of political unrest across the globe. Plus, on a personal level, we are all dealing with emotional conflicts that trigger biochemical reactions in our bodies and minds. According to an article in *Health* magazine, *"Whether a person is being stalked by a mountain lion or* [overwhelmed] *by concern for a sick loved one, the same internal defense mechanisms kick into gear . . .* [which] *involves 'every vital organ and function. . . .'"*[69] There is no exception. Every day, videos are uploaded to the internet of people having meltdowns. The COVID-19 pandemic and political pandemonium have everyone fighting on two fronts: It seems there is no end in sight.

When an issue seems to persist—for months, even years—it affects all parts of a person's being: spirit, soul, and body. Someone might argue that *true* Christians should not experience such issues. The Bible disagrees:

When hope's dream seems to drag on and on, the delay can be depressing.

---

[69] Markham Heid, "Managing Stress," *Health*, 2021, Special Edition, 10-15.

But when at last your dream comes true, life's sweetness will satisfy your soul.

—PROVERBS 13:12 TPT

Christ Jesus knows the pain of repeated disappointments intimately. He knows the anguish of personal conflicts with family, friends, and others: "Jesus...has already been tested in every way that we are tested" (Hebrews 4:15 Voice). Thus, when stressful situations continue to mount in our lives, if we are not yielding ourselves to the Spirit of Christ, then we will experience what medical experts call *amygdala hijack.*[70]

First, I will explain the term *amygdala hijack.* Psychologist Daniel Goleman coined this term to describe an emotional response that is immediate, overwhelming, and out of measure with the actual stimulus [that is, a given situation] because it has triggered a much more significant emotional threat.[71] The amygdala is the part of the brain's limbic system that defines and regulates our emotions. It also preserves memories and attaches our memories to specific emotions. For example, a person passing by a bakery shop inhales a whiff of freshly baked bread, triggering happy childhood memories. Or, if a person has experienced some form of abuse growing up, then any person resembling the abuser will trigger memories filled with fear and

---

[70] Daniel Goleman's 1996 book *Emotional Intelligence: Why It Can Matter More Than IQ.*

[71] "Conflict and Your Brain aka The Amygdala Hijacking" (PDF) Retrieved 04-07-2022

anger. Those are examples of emotional remembrances[72] that everyone experiences in every day of life. In laypeople's language, this hijack takes place when our emotions are so charged with unpleasant memories that we become irrational in our behavior toward others. We have an immediate lack of emotional control. All the Scripture readings, days of fasting, hours of prayer, and study of self-help books seem to be a distant memory as the confronting issue becomes more threatening.

Again, we all have experienced the impairment of our ability to think clearly and somberly. We know that it is right to go to God in prayer, as the Bible does teach us that we should always pray and not give up (see Luke 18:1); however, that is easier said than done. (I know this from personal experience.) For example, during the first part of the year 2021, due to the COVID-19 restrictions, I could not return from the United States of America to Barcelona, Spain, where my husband and I have lived since 2018. I traveled to the States on December 2, 2020, to be with my son. He had been diagnosed with COVID-19 and pneumonia and admitted to the intensive care unit (ICU) at the University of California San Francisco (UCSF).

Before my son's medical emergency, my husband and I had been harassed by a schizophrenic neighbor throughout the entirety of the COVID lockdown. He shouted profanity at us and curses at our God. Throughout the day and well into the

---

[72] The term "emotional remembrances" is borrowed from this website: https://www.healthline.com/health/stress/amygdala-hijack.

night, he would bang on the adjacent walls of the two apartments. Repeatedly, he spat on our apartment door, threw broken glass at it, and carved demonic symbols into it. We endured many restless days and sleepless nights during that time.

In addition to all this, a month before my son was diagnosed with COVID-19, my eighty-eight-year-old father had been hospitalized with the virus. During the same time, my husband and I lost several dear friends to this deadly pandemic. Things only seemed to worsen. In January 2021, I stayed with a relative as a houseguest. I was shocked and blindsided by my host as she verbally unleashed decades of pent-up anger toward me. She talked over me and attacked my character whenever I tried to respond to her verbal attacks. It was painful on every level. The insanity of it all is that she claimed to be directed by God. I tried to pray while the attack continued for about forty-five minutes, but to no avail.

For me, stress was turning into distress, and I did not know how to handle all the issues confronting me. Yes, I prayed, but it was difficult. My emotions ran the gamut: from sadness, hope, and regret to compassion, anger, and disappointment. I was on an emotional roller coaster, and I needed the Holy Spirit's help. I wanted God's will. My mind was exhausted. My emotions were spent. I left my relative's house the next day, vowing never to return. I was angry at the relative. I thought of all the times we had laughed, prayed, and enjoyed life together. Just a year before this incident, I had physically helped my relative change her living environment. (She lived in the chaos of clutter.) Countless times I celebrated her accomplishments. Nevertheless, I had no idea that she had held a distorted image of me, which she now demanded that I fix. What! How was I responsible for her inability to forgive? How could I not have known her true feelings?

The truth is that neither you nor I have ever been completely honest with others regarding our true feelings. We are not even honest with ourselves about our emotions and thoughts. Have any of us delved into the reasons why we react negatively to others in knee-jerk reactions? Arguably, a hundred percent of all the issues you and I will face in our lives will always involve at least one other person. If you and I have hidden issues with other people, and those people have hidden problems with us, then it stands to reason that none of us can know what is necessary for any given circumstance.

It is not that you and I are intrinsically dishonest because we do not divulge our true feelings. The unwillingness to be completely honest is a defense mechanism: *self-preservation.* Although my host told me how she felt about me, she was not honest about her feelings with herself. What were the hidden issues that fueled her meltdown—jealousy, unforgiveness, insecurity, or all the above? I do not know. Remember the warden and jailers in *The Count of Monte Cristo?* They would have handled the situation differently if they had known that Edmond was in the body bag and not the dead priest.

Regarding the incident with my relative, I decided to take the path of forgiveness, but it was rough. I am human, after all, and my emotions were raging. I did not know *how, what,* or *why* I should pray. Should I pray that the relationship would be restored? Did I want the relationship restored? The prayed-up part of me wanted restoration; however, the I-am-still-human part of me was gearing up to *Let's Just Fix This Now.* I needed help, and I needed it fast. Thank God, I yielded to the Holy Spirit. He has helped me in such trying times. It is wonderful to know that the Holy Spirit has taken all my pleas, questions, and emotions and reconciled them to the whole plan of God for my life. I could have never done that on my own because my overcharged emotions were hijacking my ability to walk in love and peace.

Scottish theologian James Denney (1856–1917)[73] assists me in summing up this chapter: "Broadly speaking, we do know what we are to pray for—the perfecting of salvation, but we do not know what we are to pray for according to what is necessary—according as the need is at the moment; we know the end, which is common to all prayers, but not what is necessary at each crisis of need in order to enable us to attain this end." The Spirit knows what is necessary in each crisis, and that is why He comes to the aid of our weakness. The purpose of this chapter is to convince you, the reader, that you will never know all there is to know about any given situation; therefore, you must depend on the Spirit of truth, who knows all there is to

---

[73] To learn about the life and works of James Denney, please follow this link: https://jasongoroncy.com/2008/07/03/james-denney-pastor-and-theologian-for-the-church/.

know about all that concerns your life. Remember the words of Christ: *"The truth-giving Spirit . . . will unveil the reality of every truth within you"* (John 16:13 TPT).[74]

The Spirit of *reality* changes everything!

---

[74] *The Passion Translation* footnote says this: "The Greek word for 'truth' is 'reality,' not 'doctrine.' It is the application of truth that matters, not just a superficial knowledge."

8

Too Deep for Words

But the Holy Spirit rises up within us to super-intercede on our behalf, pleading to God with emotional sighs too deep for words.

—ROMANS 8:26 TPT

*H*ave you ever experienced a situation that was overwhelming to the extent that no words could adequately express what you were thinking and feeling? I have. In those inexpressible moments, all I could do was sigh, moan, or groan: at times, all the above. Romans 8:26 addresses those times when words are inadequate to express our hearts' desires. In those troubling times when we are lost for words, the Spirit offers our sighs, moans, and groans to God. Those emotional sounds are laden with hidden intents, hopes, and fears. "Although we have no very definite conception of what we desire and cannot state it in a fit language (as we ought) in our prayer but only disclose it by inarticulate groanings, yet God receives these groanings as acceptable prayers inasmuch as they come from a soul full of the Holy Spirit" (Wuest).

We all have conveyed messages to other people with just a sigh or moan. A sigh can be so full of emotion that, in volume, it rivals Leo Tolstoy's *War and Peace*. For instance, when my dear husband, Larry, has done or said something that I did not like, my harrumphs—that is, the clearing of my throat—can drive him *up the wall*, figuratively. He needs at least thirty minutes to *emotionally* read what I conveyed in a single sound. The hidden message in my sigh is punctuated with quotations, questions, and exclamation marks, plus underscoring, highlighting, and capitalization. Before judging me, think about the many times you have done the same. Family, friends, and the not-so-friendlies can understand and respond to our wordless sounds. How much more the Father, Son, and Holy Spirit are able to (and do) understand all our expressed and unexpressed hearts' desires.

The triune God will receive our sighs, moans, and groans as acceptable prayers because those heart-filled emotions go beyond all utterance. I know that to be true. In 1969, when I was barely twenty-one years old, I purchased my first car. It was a beige 1965 Plymouth Barracuda. I was proud of myself and decided to visit my aunt to show off my car. While visiting my aunt, her son and a few of his friends came by her house. She was surprised to see him, and so was I, because he had some troubling personal issues. Unfortunately, while I was there, he took my car keys and left with his friends without my consent. I was upset and frightened. As I sat in my aunt's kitchen, inwardly I moaned these words, "Mother, help!" (Those were the days before cell phones.) Within ten minutes of my wordless cry, my cousin brought my car back and handed me the keys.

I grabbed my keys and ran out of the house without even saying goodbye to my aunt. I was too shaken to go back to my apartment, so I went to my mother's house. As soon as I walked into the house, my mother asked if I was okay. After explaining to her what had happened at my aunt's house, she said to me, "Loretta, I know, because about thirty minutes ago, I was in the kitchen preparing dinner when I heard your voice scream, *Mother, help!* Immediately, I fell to my knees and began to pray for you." That incident is just one example of many experiences I have had proving to me that God accepts, as a heartfelt prayer, my sighs and groans when I can find no words to express myself. And He is not a respecter of persons; what He has done for me, He will do for you.

God's acceptance of our hearts' sighs
changes everything!

9

And Then We Know

And we know [with great confidence] that God [who is deeply concerned about us] causes all things to work together [as a plan] for good for those who love God, to those who are called according to His plan and purpose.

—Romans 8:28 AMP

When we pray, the Holy Spirit helps us to expect a favorable outcome, regardless of what has happened, what is happening, or what will happen in our lives because we love God and because we are called according to God's purpose. That assertion seems to imply that our successes in life are contingent on the degree of our love for God. While it is true that we are to love the Lord God with everything that is within us,[75] it is intimidating to have our successes solely based on our track records of obeying God: To love God is to obey God. We human beings have *feet of clay*.[76] We have flaws and foibles. And those flaws affect our ability to love others—even God—unconditionally. Case in point, when we enjoy life's successes, we praise God for His greatness. Yet, when we experience life's disappointments, we blame God and question His love for us. That is an attack on God's character.

Unconditional love never attacks the character of the one who is loved. When we tell God that we love Him, and then we question His willingness to help us, that is flawed love. The Bible states that *love always believes the best*.[77] There may be those who would protest that a child of God is not flawed, but such a protest is unfounded given the Scriptures. Psalm 103:14 states that God knows that we are weak and come from dust. In Matthew 26:41, Jesus told His disciples that although their spirits are willing, their humanity is frail. Again, we are human beings who need help. Why else would Christ, before He went to the cross, pray to the Father to send us in His stead another Comforter (Helper) if we did not need help? Remember what Christ said to Peter: "But

---

[75] See Deuteronomy 6:5; 11:13; Joshua 22:5; Matthew 22:37; Mark 12:30; Luke 10:27; and Ephesians 6:24.

[76] *Feet of clay* is an expression that refers to a weakness or character flaw. This expression may have its origin from the Book of Daniel – see Daniel 2:33.

[77] "Love is a safe place of shelter, for it never stops believing the best" (1 Corinthians 13:7 TPT).

I have prayed . . . that your faith will hold firm and that you will recover from your failure and become a source of strength for your brothers here" (Luke 22:32 Voice).

Regarding Romans 8:28, the nineteenth-century Bible scholar Henry Alford (1810–1871)[78] wrote, "In this further description, the apostle designates the believers as not merely loving God, *but being beloved by God.*" Alford's commentary asserts that the guarantee of all things working out for our good is secured by the divine coupling of *loving God* and *being beloved by God.* Praise God that our security from failure is not based on our ability alone. We can depend on the love of God to carry us through the steps to success in our lives. We have hope in Christ Jesus that God's perfect and endless love will undergird us, despite our failings.

A classic example of the undergirding of God's love is the story of Abram (who later became Abraham). In the twelfth chapter of Genesis, God told Abram to leave his country, his father's home, and his relatives and travel to a foreign land. God promised Abram *special* blessings, and that He would protect him and his wife from anyone who would try to harm them. God made an unconditional promise of love and protection to Abram:

Now the LORD had said unto Abram, Get thee out of thy country, and from thy kindred, and from thy father's house, unto a land that I will shew thee: and I will make

---

[78] To learn more about Henry Alford's life and work, go to https://www.hymnologyarchive.com/henry-alford.

*of thee a great nation, and I will bless thee, and make thy
name great; and thou shalt be a blessing: and I will bless
them that bless thee, and curse him that curseth thee: and
in thee shall all families of the earth be blessed.*

—GENESIS 12:1–3

Abram did not fully trust God, because he took relatives
with him,[79] and on two separate occasions, he sold his wife,
Sarai, to a foreign ruler to protect himself.[80] Now, that is a
severe character flaw, to sacrifice a loved one in order to save
your own skin. (Note: Christ did the opposite; He sacrificed His
life to save our lives.)[81]

Yet what did God do in response to Abram's distrust and
disobedience? He saved Abram's marriage by warning the two
foreign rulers to return Sarai to Abram. One ruler's entire family
was plagued with diseases. The other ruler was threatened with
immediate death. It was Abram's distrust of God's promises that
placed both rulers and their families in jeopardy. Yet, God kept
His promises to Abram. Every bit of the wealth from the two
sales of Sarai, Abram kept. Regarding the relatives, God blessed
and saved their lives because of Abram. Plus, there had to be
some type of emotional healing for Sarai, as her safety had been
such a low priority to Abram.

---

[79] See Genesis 12:4–5. Abram took his nephew Lot, and Lot's family, with him.

[80] In Genesis 12:10–16, Abram sold his wife to Pharaoh, and in Genesis 20:1–2,
he sold his wife to the Philistine king.

[81] See Romans 5:6–10

Many people quote Deuteronomy 28:1–14 as a list of the *blessings of Abraham*. I beg to differ with them, because the promises found in Deuteronomy are contingent on the behavior of the children of Israel; however, the promise given to Abram in Genesis 12 was contingent on *God's* promises. If the promises of blessings to Abram (later named Abraham) were dependent on his obedience to God, he would have lost his marriage, his wealth, and possibly his life. The book of Deuteronomy[82] was a review of the Torah, which means "law" in Hebrew. You see, Moses gave us *rules* to live by, but Jesus the Anointed offered us the *gifts* of grace and truth. Through the grace of Christ, we have the *blessings promised to Abraham*:

> *Jesus Christ dissolved the curse from our lives, so that in him all the blessings of Abraham can be poured out upon gentiles. And now through faith we receive the promised Holy Spirit who lives in us.*
>
> —GALATIANS 3:14 TPT

The *"blessings of Abraham"* do not have the rhetoric of "if 'a,' then 'b,' but if not 'a,' then not 'b,'" but the law of Moses does. Just for the record, in no way, form, or fashion do I condone willful, habitual disobedience to God's will. I do know that out of fear, we often choose to do the very opposite of what God has told us to do. Despite our missteps, one of the *blessings of*

---

[82] Follow this web link for a short video explaining the purpose of the book of Deuteronomy: https://youtu.be/q5QEH9bH8AU.

Abraham is the divine security that all things will work out for our good because we are the *beloved of God*—our success in life is based on what God has done by the blood of Christ through the agency of the Holy Spirit. This truth bears repeating: We are sure that the plan of salvation is at work in our lives concerning all life's issues because we love God and because we are beloved by God. The love of God is unfailing, even when we fail.

The latter part of Romans 8:28 states: *"For good for those who love God, to those who are called according to His plan and purpose"* (AMP). The word *called* is the "working, in us, of the everlasting purpose of God" (Wuest), which can include *a call* to a ministry or the mission field. God continued to work His plan in Abraham and Sarah so that they were eventually heralded as champions of faith, enjoying the realization of their hearts' desires (see Hebrews 11:8–12). God is perfecting the *call of salvation in our lives.* He designed this plan before the very foundations of the world were laid. Even before the fall, God determined that He would, in Christ, through the Holy Spirit, cause all things to work for our good despite our weaknesses if we depend on the Holy Spirit's help.

The Spirit of love changes everything!

Conclusion

The Spirit of Truth, Our Helper

*Y*es, we are free moral agents. We have the freedom either to choose or to reject God's will for our lives. When we decide to make decisions without the Holy Spirit's help, we can cause harm to others and ourselves. If the jailers in Alexandre Dumas' *The Count of Monte Cristo* had known that Edmond Dantès was in the body bag instead of the dead priest, they would have handled the situation quite differently. True, Edmond is the heroic protagonist of Dumas' novel. Readers are thrilled at Edmond's escape from prison. Nevertheless, the jailers caused the warden's death because they acted on their preconceptions of the situation. The jailers discovered that Faria, the priest, had died. They placed the dead priest in a body bag. They left the body in the jail cell to go and tell the warden of the death. The jailers returned with the warden. They assumed the dead priest was still in the body bag; there was no reason to think differently. But things had changed dramatically between the time the jailers left the dead priest's cell and when they returned to it with the warden: Edmond had traded places with the dead priest.

Our lives often seem to be in a constant state of flux: Everything familiar to us can change instantly. Our preconceived notions about a given circumstance can be as useless as a flat tire. We must decide to yield to the ministry of the Holy Spirit because He comes to our rescue by reconciling our hearts' cries to God's plan for us. As Jesus said, "Howbeit when he, the Spirit of truth, is come, he will guide you into all truth" (John 16:13).

Now the Spirit of truth changes everything!

Works Cited

Wuest, Kenneth S. *Word Study in the Greek New Testament.* Grand Rapids: Wm. B. Eerdman's Publishing, Grand Rapids, 1945.

Heid, Markham. "Rising To The Challenge." *Health* (2021): 10-15.

About the Author

Loretta Huggins is a wife, a mother, and a grandmother. She earned a bachelor's degree in English after enjoying a successful career in the fashion industry. She has traveled to twenty-five countries and thirty-eight of the fifty states of the USA. She now resides in Spain, where she and her husband, Larry Huggins, co-pastor ZChurch, a Spirit-filled, international, online church. She is a compelling and entertaining public speaker who loves history, literature, and the arts.

Contact Info

Loretta Huggins
5655 Silver Creek Valley Rd., #106
San Jose, CA 95138 USA

email: lorettahuggins8@gmail.com

url: https://zchurch.life/

Recommended Reading

By Larry Huggins:

The Blood Speaks

The Cup of Blessings

The Easy Way to Walk in the Spirit

The Real You (co-authored by Bernal and Huggins)